One barrel cactus
in the desert.

Two barrel cacti
in the desert.

Three prickly pears
in the desert.

Four prickly pears
in the desert.

Five Christmas cacti
in the desert.

Six Christmas cacti
in the desert.

Seven chollas
in the desert.

Eight chollas
in the desert.

Nine saguaros
in the desert.

Ten saguaros
in the desert.

See the cacti in the desert
on this beautiful day.

1

2

3

4

5

6

7

8

9

10